ON THE QUAYS

On The Quays presents

Stop/Over
by Gary Duggan

Dublin Fringe Festival
10–23 September 2018
Chocolate Factory Dublin

Stop/Over
by Gary Duggan

CAST

F	Siobhán Callaghan
M	Ashleigh Dorrell

COMPANY

Director	Nicola Murphy
Lighting Designer	Eoin Lennon
Scenic Designer & Costume Designer	Jack Scullion
Sound Designer	Denis Clohessy
Production Manager	Líadan Ní Chearbhaill
Production Stage Manager	Rachael Kivlehan
Assistant Stage Manager	Grace Halton
Assistant Director	Matt Engle
Music Director & Supervisor, Producer	Keiji Ishiguri
Executive Producer	Michael Quadrino
Business Manager	AnLi Kelly-Durham
Social Media Supervisors	Jenna Tanzola & AnLi Kelly-Durham
Press Representative	Dan DeMello

Stop/Over is funded through an Arts Council Theatre Project Award.

BIOGRAPHIES

Siobhán Callaghan – F

Siobhán Callaghan is an Irish actor and a graduate from The Lir National Academy of Dramatic Art. During her time at The Lir she played parts such as Christine in Tom Stoppard's *Dalliance* directed by Hilary Wood, various characters in *Incognito* by Nick Payne directed by Ronan Leahy, the Messenger in *Thyestes* directed by Annabelle Comyn and Widow Quin in *The Playboy of The Western World* directed by Caitríona McLaughlin.

Prior to The Lir, Siobhán performed in a sold-out run of *Coppers Uncovered: The Walk of Shame* in The Underbelly Theatre and *Keeping Abreast*, directed by Michael Scott in The Assembly Theatre in The Edinburgh Fringe Festival.

She also played various characters in *A Sense of Keane*, pulling from the work of John B. Keane, directed by Michael Scott in the Civic Theatre.

Her film credits include *Streetcar* directed by Laura Way and *The Late Men* directed by Van Poynton. She is also a graduate of Bull Alley Theatre Training Company.

Ashleigh Dorrell – M

Theatre credits include: Mae in Ciara Elizabeth Smyth's award-winning *All Honey*, Brigit in Katie McCann's *The Grimm Tale of Cinderella*, Lydia Languish in Richard Brinsley Sheridan's *The Rivals*, Sarah Walters in Ian Toner's *Animalia*, Anne Brontë and Cathy Earnshaw in Polly Teale's *Brontë*, Woman in Philip Ridely's *Tender Napalm*, Paige Turner in Theatre Lovett's *The Absurd Cat Quiz* and Meg March in Teri FitzGerald's *The Wise Wound*.

Film work includes *Nightshift* by Steve Hall and Greenflash Pictures.

She was nominated for Best Performer at the Dublin Fringe Awards, for *Animalia*, which won the Stewart Parker BBC NI Radio Drama Award, the Fishamble New Writing Award and was nominated for the Bewley's Little Gem Award.

Ashleigh is a graduate of The Gaiety School of Acting.

Gary Duggan – Writer

Gary Duggan is an award-winning playwright, screenwriter and director.

His first play, *Monged* (Fishamble, Dublin, also Belgrade Theatre, Coventry), won the Stewart Parker Trust Award. A film adaptation premiered at the 2015 Galway Film Fleadh.

Other plays include: *Dedalus Lounge* (Pageant Wagon, Dublin, Royal Family Productions, New York); *Mission* (Origin, New York & Theatre Upstairs, Dublin); *Trans-Euro Express* (Pageant Wagon, Dublin; Fundamental Theater Company/ Irish Arts Centre, New York); *Neuropolis* (Dublin Fringe Festival 2010) and *It's a Wonderful Bleeding Life* (Theatre Upstairs & Bewley's Café Theatre). *Shibari* (Abbey Theatre, Dublin) premiered at the 2012 Dublin Theatre Festival. His most recent play, *Run / Don't Run* (Bigger Picture Projects), had a national tour in 2015.

After *Stop/Over*, Gary's next play, *Spotless*, will premiere in 2019. He has participated in devised work with Anu, Theatre Upstairs and the Gaiety School in Dublin and workshopped plays with The Irish Arts Centre and The Irish Rep in New York.

Gary also works in film and TV. He recently directed the short films *Shoebox* and *Inner Child*, and *Costigan*, a crime drama pilot for RTÉ's Storyland, which is currently being developed into a full series. Gary co-wrote the much talked about drama, *Amber*, which premiered on RTÉ and BBC4 in 2014. The mini-series sold to multiple territories throughout the world.

Gary has been commissioned three times by the Abbey Theatre (National Theatre of Ireland) and currently has two features in development with Screen Ireland along with several other film and TV projects attached to Irish and international production companies.

Nicola Murphy – Director, Co-Founder of On The Quays

Nicola is a director, actress and producer. She is a graduate of The American Academy of Dramatic Arts and received her MFA in Directing from The Lir, National Academy of Dramatic Art, Trinity College Dublin. Previous directing credits include: the premiere production of *Rent* at Cas Di Cultura, Aruba's National Theatre, this production also performed a sold-out run at The Edinburgh Festival Fringe; the world premiere of *Beef* by Michael Musi, at The Box Theatre in Toronto; the short film *FLOAT* (co-directed); *The Events* by David Greig at The Lir Academy; *Alone With Friends* at Holiday House NYC; and *Mighty Atoms* at The American Academy of Dramatic Arts. Assistant Directing credits include *Katie Roche* at The Abbey; *Silence is Requested* at The Lir Academy; working with Shirley Knight on Sir Peter Shaffer's *Five Finger Exercise* celebration reading at The Players Club NYC; *Trans-Euro Express* at The Irish Arts Centre; and& an assistantship placement with Neal Street Productions on the hit UK show *Call The Midwife* (BBC & PBS). She is a faculty member teaching artist on New Jersey Performing Arts Center's arts education program, and member of The Young Vic Director's Program, London. *Stop/Over* marks her professional directorial debut in Dublin.

Eoin Lennon – Lighting Design
Eoin began his foray into all things stage and lighting design at Trinity College Dublin. While studying Theoretical Physics he quickly became embroiled in theatre as a challenging creative outlet. Since then he has enjoyed a colourful experience working around Ireland on a variety of projects from dance and devising to music and performance art. Eoin's previous work with Dublin Fringe Festival includes *Fierce Notions*, *Dummy*, *These Lights* and *Birdy* ('17), *Mimes in Time* ('16), and *Remember to Breathe* ('15). Other recent credits include *Walkinstown* (Smock Alley Theatre) and *Minding Frankie* (Gaiety Theatre, national tour). He has recently returned after a successful tour of *Giselle* (Edinburgh Fringe Festival).

Jack Scullion – Set & Costume Design
Jack has studied theatre and design at NUI Galway and UC Santa Barbara, and is a recent graduate of the MFA in Stage Design at The Lir. His recent credits include costume for *Incognito* at The Lir; set and costume for *Pests* at the Clonmel Junction Festival; *I See You* in Theatre Upstairs; and *After the End* in the Lyric and New Theatre.

Denis Clohessy – Sound Designer
Denis has worked with many dance and theatre companies including The Abbey Theatre, The Gate Theatre, Rough Magic, Junk Ensemble, Fishamble and The Corn Exchange. He won the Irish Times Theatre Award in 2011 and composed the music for Pat Kinevane's 2016 Olivier winning play *Silent* (Fishamble). He also composes music extensively for film and television including *Older than Ireland* (Snackbox Films); *The Land of the Enlightened* (Fastnet Films) and *His and Hers* (Venom Film).

Líadan Ní Chearbhaill – Production Manager
Líadan Ní Chearbhaill is a production manager with a background in stage management and lighting. She has been involved in technical theatre since 2012 when she joined Maynooth University Drama Society. She is currently participating in Rough Magic SEEDS programme. Recent production and stage management credits include *Efficacy 84* (Dublin Fringe Festival 2017); *it's getting harder and harder for me* (Dublin Fringe Festival 2017); as well as assistant stage manager for *This Beach* (Brokentalkers national tour 2017).

Rachael Kivlehan – Production Stage Manager
Rachael is a recent Stage Management and Technical Theatre graduate of The Lir Academy. During her time at The Lir she stage managed *The Skriker* directed by Tom Creed, *The Winter's Tale* directed by Nona Shepphard, and *The Caucasian Chalk Circle* directed by Tom Creed. Outside of college, Rachael has stage managed on *The Aeneid* (Collapsing Horse, Dublin Fringe 2016); and *Absolute Legends* (THISISPOPBABY/Lords of Strut, Dublin Fringe 2017).

Grace Halton – Assistant Stage Manager

Grace Halton (A.L.C.M) is a freelance theatre practitioner based in Dublin. Grace has a keen interest in promenade performances having worked on *School for Scandal* in Dublin Castle; *The Secret Garden* in Rathfarnham Castle and *The Adventures of Alice* in Pearse Museum. Grace also teaches Speech, Drama and Mime in Betty Ann Norton Theatre School. Grace is in her second year of studying Stage Management and Technical Theatre at The Lir Academy.

Matt Engle – Assistant Director, Co-Founder of On The Quays

Matt Engle's theatrical career may have peaked at the age of five, when he was cast as the title character in his kindergarten class's production of *The Gingerbread Boy*, but that doesn't mean he's done trying. After earning his BFA in theater performance from Hofstra University, he has worked in a variety of roles both off and on the stage, in NYC and abroad. He assistant directed a sold-out run of *Rent* at the 2015 Edinburgh Fringe Festival and most recently co-produced *A Play About Drew Carey*, a new original work. He is a member of the artistic team for WalkUpArts, a developing production company. As an actor, he has performed in the FRIGID Festival and the Edinburgh Fringe Festival. Favorite credits include: Juliet in *Romeo/Juliet* (a movement-based adaptation of the classic), Gerry/Joshua in *Cloud Nine*, and Matthew Hudlocke in *The Marriage of Bette and Boo*.

Keiji Ishiguri – Music Director & Supervisor, Co-Founder of On The Quays

Keiji is a professional music director, pianist, arranger, composer and teacher throughout New York City and Westchester. In addition to his role as resident music director of On The Quays, he has vocal coached and music directed for Pace University, Ars Nova, the Lucy Moses School at the Kaufman Center, Crestwood Music Education Center, PlayGroup Theater, Brooklyn Friends School, and the Beacon School. A graduate of Yale University where he music directed such groups as the Whiffenpoofs, Keiji also continues to lead a cappella ensembles, including the semi-professional Lost Keys of New York. Keiji is also an avid vocal arranger, his pieces having been performed throughout the world and on such TV shows as *Glee*! His recently published Book of Rounds – 21 epiphanal pieces written in conjunction with songwriters Julie Flanders and Emil Adler is available on iTunes and Spotify.

Michael Quadrino – Executive Producer, Co-Founder of On The Quays

Michael has been involved in the arts for most of his life. A competitive figure skater for 18 years, he has numerous accomplishments as a skater and is an actor and producer. He also spent many years directing and choreographing many ice shows in New York. A graduate of Hofstra University in 2012, Michael has a B.S. in Exercise Science and a minor in Drama. After graduating, Michael co-produced a production of *Romeo and Juliet* at the 2013 Edinburgh Festival Fringe with some fellow Hofstra students entitled *Romeo/Juliet*. It was that incredible experience that led him to keep wanting to produce shows at the festival. In 2015, he co-produced a production of *Rent* at the Edinburgh Festival Fringe with Nicola Murphy directing the production. This production enjoyed a sold-out run and 5-star reviews at the festival. Since co-founding On The Quays he reprised his role in *Rent* which OTQ produced in Aruba for the first time in October 2017.

AnLi Kelly-Durham – Business Manager for On The Quays
AnLi Kelly-Durham is thrilled to be joining the team at On The Quays. Following her acting debut in her community youth theatre's one-act play festival, AnLi decided she was better suited for the business side of theatre. Recently, she co-produced *Rent* at Cas Di Cultura in Aruba with On The Quays and Janet Krupin's Chemical Drive at Feinstein's/54 Below. AnLi is a graduate of American University and currently works as a public relations professional in the financial industry.

Jenna Tanzola – Producer, Co-Founder of On The Quays
Jenna Tanzola is a co-founder and director of On The Quays, with a BFA in theatre arts from Hofstra University. She's excited to continue telling genuine stories as part of such an incredible line-up. Jenna hopes to continue her multi-faceted work in theater while also diving headfirst into the marketing industry. Right now she's gearing up to co-host an event to celebrating a new drag haus. Catch her there or behind the scenes of some of the OTQ social media posts!

Dan DeMello – Press Agent
Dan DeMello has coordinated publicity campaigns in United States, Canada, London, Germany, India and Ireland. He's represented hundreds of Off-Broadway productions and dozens of galas and events. Current clients include: On the Quays, Harlem Repertory Theatre, Wheelhouse Theater Company, Crash Theater Company, New York Deaf Theatre, The 1st Annual Trump Family Special, The Theater Center in Times Square and NYC's longest running play, Perfect Crime. In addition to his theatrical clients, he represents SCRUFF, the preeminent global gay social networking, dating and travel app with more than 12 million members worldwide.

On The Quays
Founded in September 2016 by a group of artists from varying backgrounds, On The Quays is an international production company based in New York City. Dedicated to creating and producing work in theatre, film, and digital media, the company are inspired to tell relevant and engaging stories that promote inclusivity, empathy and understanding. In 2017 the company produced the premiere production of Jonathan Larson' rock opera *Rent* at Cas Di Cultura, Aruba's National Theatre. In 2018 they will produce Gary Duggan's *Stop/Over* as part of The Dublin Fringe Festival.

STOP/OVER

Gary Duggan

An earlier version of *Stop/Over* had a workshop performance at Solstice as part of the Cork Midsummer Festival in June 2011, with the following cast:

M	Sam Peter Corry
F	Aoibhin Garrihy
Director	Gavin Logue

An abridged version of *Stop/Over* had a rehearsed reading as part of the 20:Love play-reading series for the Abbey Theatre, Dublin, in 2008, with the following cast:

M	Paul Reid
F	Lisa Lambe
Director	Rachel West

Acknowledgements

Thanks to:

All my collaborators on earlier versions of the play: Jimmy Fay, Sam Peter Corry, Gemma Reeves, Aideen Howard, Jessica Traynor, Rachel West, Paul Reid, Lisa Lambe, David Horan, Gavin Logue, Aoibhin Garrihy, Liam Heslin, Leah Minto.

Ruth McGowan and all at Dublin Fringe Festival, Nick Quinn at The Agency, London, and all at the Arts Council for their support for the project.

Nicola Murphy, for her faith and passion in the play over a number of years. And all at On The Quays for their dedication, commitment and hard work (across time zones) on the premiere production.

My parents, John and Mary; and Aenne Barr, for all their continued love and support.

G.D.

Characters

M, *twenties*
F, *twenties*

The play is set...

in a moment of eye contact, now...

and in New York, years ago...

Author's Note

This play is short and fast.

The audience should feel as though they've been dropped right into the middle of the city and that they are always a step or two behind the narrators. They must jog to keep up.

There should be some sort of constant soundtrack (sound FX and/or music), a feeling of the city and the couple's memories and adrenalin rising and falling all around us.

Staging and design are completely at the director's discretion.

The character of 'M' can be played by either a man or a woman. At a couple of points in dialogue, there is alternate gender-specific words/phrases within square brackets.

This text went to press before the end of rehearsals and so may differ slightly from the play as performed.

A Crossing

M. Walking today. Just walking. No hurry. No particular destination. Hand-in-hand with my girlfriend. Not talking. Just walking. Content. Ordinary. Nothing...

F. Until?

M. I see her.

F. Her?

M. Yes.

F. Who?

M. You.

F. Me. Just here. Waiting.

M. For what?

F. Just waiting.

M. For who?

F. A lover? My brother? My husband? Someone. No one you know.

M. No one I know?

F. No.

M. I know you.

F. Yes?

M. Yeah.

F. It takes a second.

M. A glint of recognition.

F. A flash.

M. A momentary glance.

F. A flush?

M. Electric eye contact that transmits everything…

F. So much.

M.…in an instant.

F. I knew you.

M. A flicker.

F. You release your girlfriend's hand for a moment.

M. A smile.

F. A reflex.

M. Hey.

F. Hi.

M. No more.

F. Just that.

M. Then moving past.

F. Girlfriend didn't even register a change.

M. But everything's changed.

F. Now.

M. Since then.

F. When?

M. I knew you.

   A beat.

F. This is now and then.

M.This is our place.

F. This is New York.

M. This is years ago.

F. Is it?

M. It is.

F. Jesus.

M. When you were young and your heart was an open book.

F. You used to say…

M. I used to say…?

A shift.

You look the same.

F. I do? Same as when?

M. Then. Last time I saw you.

F. Not older?

M. No. You haven't changed.

F. I never change. Scary, huh?

M. A little…

F. I would have liked to stay for longer.

M. I know. It's okay. I'm just glad to see you now.

F. That's good. Me to.

M. We're gonna have a great… thirty-one hours… or whatever. I've everything sorted. You can just put yourself in my hands for the next while. Can you do that?

F. I think so.

M. I hate the airport.

F. How do we get out of here?

M. Shuttle bus to the subway.

A shift.

My place is on Avenue A.

F. Ah, Alphabet City.

M. That's right. Guy in a bar told me a little ditty about Alphabet City.

F. Oh yeah?

M. Yeah. *On Avenue A, you're alright. On B, you're brave. On C, you're crazy. And on D, you're dead.*

F. Nice.

M. Yeah, well, it's not as rough as it used to be apparently.

F. Orange and red chimneys protrude from roadworks running along the middle of the street, letting out thick clouds of smoke and steam.

M. There is the steady tune of police and ambulance sirens and honking car horns, rising and falling all around us like some insane music.

F. Is it always like this?

M. Yeah.

F. Crazy how intense just walking down the street feels in New York.

M. It's like someone's taken the city and cranked the volume and atmosphere all the way up. Some dangerous experiment.

F. We go to this deli. *Best* bagels in New York.

M. You been here before?

F. No.

M. How do you know that then?

F. Says it on the wall there.

M. Well, they are pretty good.

F. I'm sure they are. Why would they lie?

M. The radio is playing Ricky fucking Martin 'Livin' La Vida fucking Loca'. Again.

F. I kinda like it.

M. What? Please be joking. It's on every time I come in here.

F. And I'm going to start humming it any time things get awkward.

M. Please, don't.

F. It's not too late to send me back to the airport.

M. I'll bear that in mind. Let's drop your bag into my place. It's just around the corner.

F. Sure.

M. I gotta warn you, there's a lot of steps.

F. That's okay, you're carrying the bag.

M's Apartment

F. You look good.

M. I do?

F. Yeah. Happy?

M. I guess, yeah. I fucking love this place.

F. You didn't feel that way in that email.

M. That was ages ago. I'd just arrived.

F. You were lonely.

M. Not really, I was…

F. You said you were lonely. An anonymous speck in the mad bad city.

M. Yeah, I suppose I felt that at first, but then…

F. But then?

M. You start to realise that being an anonymous speck in the mad bad city is pretty fucking liberating.

F. It is?

M. Oh yeah. Trouble with Dublin, with Ireland, is, you can't move without bumping into someone you know.

F. The morning after a night on coke or something and here's your auntie coming out of SuperValu.

M. Exactly. No escape. Over here it's different.

F. Clean slate. Blank page.

M. More people between here and Harlem than in the whole of Ireland. The population of our entire country wedged into about a hundred and twenty city blocks. Think about it.

F. Crazy when you put it like that.

M. I love it. Takes a little bit of getting used to. But when you do. You feel like you can do anything. *Be* anything. Say what you want. Wear what you want. Do what you want. No one's going to criticise you. Or take the piss. Or slag you off.

F. You don't miss that lovely homegrown scent of good ol' Irish begrudgery?

M. No, fuck that! I'll give you an example. On my way to work every day I pass this guy selling sunglasses. Thing about this guy is, he's wearing nothing but a leather thong and a pair of rollerblades. No one bats an eyelid at him.

F. Unless they wanna buy a pair of sunglasses.

M. Exactly, I fucking love that.

F. So you love New York because of the semi-naked sunglass vendors.

M. Yeah, I suppose. In a way.

Pause.

This is nice. I like this.

F. What?

M. This little banter. Easy and casual, like we just seen each other yesterday.

F. Why wouldn't it be? Hasn't been that long, has it?

M. Ah, a lot can happen in a year.

F. Yeah. I guess.

M. I've made a plan.

F. For what?

M. For us. For now. Tonight.

F. You didn't have to.

M. What are you talking about? Of course I did.

F. I wasn't expecting anything.

M. You're in New York for one night.

F. You didn't have to go to any trouble.

M. It wasn't any trouble. It's going to be great.

F. What exactly have you planned?

M. You said you'd put yourself in my hands.

F. That depends.

M. You're going to love it.

F. Okay...

M. You gotta see some of the city, don't you?

F. Maybe I do. But I wasn't expecting this. I don't know what I was expecting. To see you. Be with you. Talk about old times. A few laughs. Take my mind off everything back home. Everything since...

M. You always were up for anything. Everything. The wildest nights. Pushing the boat out. Finding the best times. I'm not going to disappoint you tonight. I'm going to show you everything. This place. All that I've found. Who I am now. Maybe then...

A shift.

You wanna take a shower?

F. That would be great.

M. You leave the door open.

F. Stiffness and stickiness from hours of travel wash away. Dull tiredness washing away. Maybe a night on the town is what I need. One last time.

M. You come out, wrapped in a towel, as I pop the cork of the Moët in celebration.

F. Just happened to have a bottle of champagne lying around?

M. For special occasions.

F. Like this?

M. Sure. I'm prepared. Bought champagne flutes in Macy's and everything.

F. And away you pour.

M. Both slouched coolly across the sofa. Sipping away.

F. Slipping away. Towel loose, hair wet.

M. Watching you rub creams into your skin.

F. Face and arms.

M. Neck and legs.

F. I thought about you the other day.

M. I feel privileged. What did you think about?

F. Some time we danced.

M. Oh yeah?

F. I wore a blue dress.

M. A blue dress?

F. Yes. Clingy. Sky blue.

M. Devil in a Blue Dress. When's this?

F. You don't remember? College.

M. When?

F. First year, I think. Some night. I danced with you.

M. *Of course* I remember dancing with you.

F. We were out.

M. Together.

F. Alone. Sort of… Not with the class.

M. No. I asked you to a thing. Asked you, without expecting, just… I don't know.

F. I didn't want to be at home then.

M. Great.

F. No. I enjoyed being with you too.

M. Hey, you're up to your knees, keep digging.

F. My mother wasn't happy then. Something was up. I'd come home and she'd be sitting in the kitchen. At the table. Sipping cups of cold tea.

M. What was wrong?

F. She wouldn't speak. I tried. I don't know. My brother? Sisters? My dad? She wouldn't speak. Just sat there. Dead smile on her face. And looking like she might cry but never actually doing it. I think, days like this. And then… I didn't want to be home any more.

M. So you came out with me. On a Tuesday.

F. A fucking Tuesday?

M. Them's was the days. I couldn't believe you agreed. Thought you were taking the piss outta me or something. I mean I was sorta taking the piss asking you but… You showed up and you looked…

F. What?

M. I don't know… like you wanted to be there. Not like, awkward. Or, just there 'cause you said you would. And regretting it now.

F. I did want to be there. Something different. Some… what was it?

M. DramaSoc night, or…

F. We danced.

M. Yeah, you wore that blue dress.

F. I thought you didn't remember that.

M. *Of course* I remember your blue dress.

F. That was the first night I really looked at you.

M. What?

F. I mean, I knew you before that. Your voice there. Talking to me. And a presence there. Whenever in college. But I never really looked at you until that night. Dancing with you.

M. And not jumping-around techno shit. Hands clasped, spinning disco shit. Bee Gees. Cheesy but, fun. What the hell, we're eighteen.

F. Nineteen.

M. Yeah.

F. I looked at your face. Your eyes. A real intense blue. Hadn't noticed them before. Almost fake, so blue.

M. Fake eyes I have now?

F. On me, intense, even when you were having a laugh. Dancing.

M. Hey, you were smiling.

F. Yeah. I was. I was happy there. Dancing with you. Where was it again?

M. You don't remember where it was?

F. No.

M. You really wanna know?

F. Yeah.

M. Gonna ruin your nice image.

F. Really?

M. Yeah. You wanna know where that was? That was in Break for the fuckin Border.

F. No!

M. Yes!

F. Fuck, really? Break for the fuckin Border?

M. Yeah. A Tuesday night. Some DramaSoc thing.

F. Fuck.

M. Ah, whatever, we were eighteen.

F. Nineteen.

> *A shift.*

> This. I'd be happy with this. Just sitting here a while.
> With you.

M. We've finished the bottle already. Don't want you getting
bored.

F. But I can see you're excited about this plan of yours.

M. Don't want you getting dragged down by everything from
before.

F. Keen to get going.

M. Want to keep you up. Take your mind off everything. Have
the buzz like back in college. But better. In New York City.

F. One night only.

M. Let's do it all.

F. Alrighty then.

> I've left a Calvin Klein dress at the top of my rucksack. It's
> my sole remaining piece of clean clothing.

M. Literally, I watch you put it on with no underwear.

F. Our little secret. When I knew I was heading home early,
I decided not to waste any time going to the laundromat.

M. Content to let everything build up for your ma's washing
machine back home.

F. I'm such a bloke.

M. Not from where I'm standing.

F. It's getting late. Get dressed.

Subway

F. You want to save us walking.

M. Two stops on the subway?

F. We duck down into the 2nd Av Station.

M. The platform's pretty busy. People heading home from work, shopping.

F. And some like us, out on the town early, dressed up.

M. Do I have something on my face?

F. No, why?

M. A few people we passed looked at me funny.

F. People?

M. Guys. People.

F. You're paranoid. Don't be paranoid.

M. No. Another guy just looked at me there. He –

F. What?

M. I get it.

F. What?

M. Three Hispanic guys on the opposite platform. Young, tough. Gold chains, Yamaha jackets slung from their shoulders.

F. Two stare across the tracks, kind of at us. The third smiles, says something. The others nod.

M. The eastbound F roars into the station blocking them from our view. They did it too.

F. Yeah?

M. They checked you out.

F. That's okay, I'm kinda used to it.

M. I suppose you are, but… They checked you out and then they looked at me.

F. So?

M. So, they looked at you, then they looked at me and thought,
'Are they together?'

F. Don't be stupid.

M. I'm not. I know that look. I've made that look myself,
looking at people on the street.

F. Don't be neurotic.

M. Sorry.

F. Where are we going now?

M. We take the M across to West 4th, then walk to one of my
favourite restaurants.

Dinner

F. A cute little place that you can sit at tables outside and watch
the Greenwich Village circus dancing merrily by.

M. I love this place, I swear the blueberry pie here [gives me
a boner / makes me wet], it's that good.

F. That's quite a recommendation.

M. Trust me, it's great. We'll have the claret.

F. You've been learning, huh?

M. Please, I've been living in Manhattan for three years. I'm
sophisticated now.

F. You keep watching me sipping my drink.

M. What have you done to your eyes?

F. Mascara. Same as always.

M. Seem different. Darker. Bigger. You have big dark eyes.

F. Same as always. Always this dark. Always this big.

M. The colossal squid has the biggest eyes of any living creature on the planet. Black and dead and round. Able to see in total blackness. See everything. See things that cannot see you. That's you, that is. You're a colossal fucking squid…

F. Not quite sure what you mean by that. Is that an insult or an honest description?

M. You think I see you as a cold, undulating sea creature?

F. I've been told I have an icy quality more than once.

M. Is it starting to worry you?

F. No. The ones who told me that have been pretty needy and I've been in no hurry to give them what they need.

M. So their opinion doesn't matter.

F. Not a bit.

M. Has it been a busy summer for you?

F. How do you mean?

M. Any adventures? Romance?

F. I wouldn't say romance. Some fooling around.

M. Some fooling around?

F. You hardly expect me to go without sex for three months?

M. No. I guess not. Who'd you fool around with?

F. Well… There was a biker, who had a Harley. We rode to San Diego on it one weekend. I think he was more interested in that bike than me.

M. Anyone else?

F. A Scottish guy. And a surfer, of course. California, after all.

M. Of course.

F. The Scottish guy had something. He was older. Experienced. Very good with his tongue.

M. Really…

F. Yeah… Nothing too memorable though. Fleeting.

M. Not like our little fling?

F. No. Not like that. Not at all.

M. That's what we're calling it then?

F. A fling?

M. Yes.

F. I don't know what you'd call it.

M. I've thought about it – us – a lot.

F. Yeah, I bet you have.

M. Jesus, you're good, aren't you?

F. Too good?

M. You'll die alone.

F. Won't we all.

A shift.

I don't tell you that the surfer was a girl. Or that the Scottish guy proposed to me. I don't think you'd find either of those things funny.

M. I don't tell you that I was in a relationship here. Last time I saw you in Dublin.

F. I don't tell you about the guy at that party I woke up having sex with and then having to get a morning-after pill and an STD test, and that I drank a full bottle of vodka by myself waiting for the results.

M. I don't tell you that seeing you then, and the way we left things, screwed everything up here.

F. I don't tell you the test came back clear. All clean. In that regard, if none other.

M. I don't tell you how long I was waiting, *willing*, for you, to get in contact again.

A shift.

F. My mother's selling the pub.

M. Oh?

F. Yeah. We thought we could hold on to it. But her heart's not into it and the guy she hired to manage the place was useless.

M. Why not get another guy?

F. No. She's made up her mind. Took her this long, but it's what she wants now. Move on somehow.

M. That's shitty. Sorry to hear that. I know that place meant so much to your family. To your dad.

F. Yeah. But he's dead now.

M. Yeah.

F. Hard to believe it's been almost a year.

M. How has your mother been?

F. As good as. She's tough. Resilient. He was much older than her. She knew it would happen some day. That she'd be left behind.

M. Yeah but, still…

F. It meant so much to me, you being there at the funeral. You didn't have to be there.

M. I was going to be in Dublin anyway.

F. I know. Seeing your family though. I never expected you there.

M. A surprise.

F. Yeah. None of my gang hung around. A lot of them didn't even come.

M. Too cool for school.

F. Too awkward for something real.

M. Like death or…

F. You came to the pub with me. Stayed with me. Not being serious. Laughing and talking. Meant a lot to me.

M. I'm glad.

F. You're stuck in some part of my head because of that.

M. I'm glad.

F. Being there for me. Again, after so long.

M. Not *that* long since college.

F. Isn't it? We barely even knew each other that well. Not so I'd expect to see you there.

M. I knew you.

F. Yeah, but…

M. Now. Then. From the very start of college. That's years.

F. From that walk?

M. What walk?

F. That time we walked across town together.

M. When we had just started?

F. Yeah. The rest of the class had got the bus, but we decided to walk.

M. All the way across town.

F. Practically canal to canal.

M. Yes. That was the first time we really spoke with each other. Got to know each other. We didn't run out of things to say once…

F. Chemistry?

M. Maybe. I suppose, yeah. We went for coffee.

F. What did we talk about?

M. Freshers' Week. *Great Expectations*. That American cunt we had psychoanalysing Red Riding Hood.

F. Boring. You remember all this?

M. Like a movie. Those were the days.

F. How many years ago?

M. Enough to know you.

   A shift.

   Walking down Bleecker Street toward 6th Avenue now.

F. We're still sipping claret from the glasses we walked away from the restaurant with.

M. I down the last drop and smash the glass in the gutter.

F. You're so bad.

M. A taxi turns the corner at the far end of Houston.

F. You're about to hail it, when we see it's already taken.

M. I decide to play matador instead.

F. Swiping the tail of your coat over the roof of the large yellow bull.

M. The driver honks angrily, disappears down 6th.

F. We collapse in a fit of drunken giggles.

M. Almost falling over each other outside S.O.B.'s

F. Before ducking back down into Christopher Street Station.

M. The subway brings us uptown to West 23rd Street. Perfect.

F. Where are we going now?

M. Right here. La Maison de Sade.

La Maison

F. What the fuck is this place?

M. It's an S&M bar.

F. An S&M bar?

M. Yeah.

F. Cool.

M. The doorman opens up for us and we move inside through a heavy velvet curtain.

F. It's pretty small inside, two rooms, one with a bar, dark sort of electro music playing at a fair volume.

M. Lots of mirrors, chrome and leather. The barman looks like one of the Village People; leather chaps and waistcoat.

F. The waitresses are very sexy and severe-looking. Tonnes of eyeshadow and dark lipstick. PVC corsets and shiny skirts.

M. We're offered a table near the bar.

F. And order two 'Masochists' from the cocktail menu.

M. Which includes a price list for various forms of abuse and punishment.

F. Bondage. Spanking. Verbal intimidation. Submissive lessons.

M. It's all a bit surreal.

F. There's a big group at a table opposite. They're having a great laugh.

M. Two of the party have requested some 'disciplining'.

F. A guy and girl, they seem to be a couple.

M. The bar guy finishes mixing our cocktails and passes them to our waitress. As she delivers the drinks to our table, the barman takes some leather handcuffs from behind the bar and moves over to the two volunteers.

F. I sip on my Masochist. It's oily black and tastes of liquorice and gin. Very potent.

M. Hmm. A dominatrix in fishnets has joined the barman in the open space in front of the bar. They are attaching the young couple to a pair of pillars using the leather cuffs.

F. Then blindfolding them. The couple facing each other. The barman takes up position behind the woman.

M. The dominatrix behind the guy. She's got an array of whips, paddles and canes. She passes some of them to the barman.

F. And they proceed to caress, squeeze and spank the living hell out of the young bound couple. Much to the enjoyment of their friends opposite.

M. What is this?

F. How do you mean?

M. Is this love, sex or violence?

F. Entertainment?

M. All of the above?

F. Well, yeah. It's like a combination of all of those things.

M. In a bar in Chelsea…

F. Love and sex, it's all a bit violent and entertaining, isn't it?

M. It is?

F. You never really enjoyed fucking someone when you were angry at them, hated them even? Enjoying the violence of it. I've left marks on people.

M. I'm sure you have.

F. For days. Bruises. Bites. Scrapes. And I've had a few myself. Sometimes you want that. Sometimes that's what feels good. What just happens.

M. Passion is violent.

Pause.

You enjoying this?

F. This? This is… I'm enjoying this cocktail. I'm enjoying the novelty, the outrageousness, of it. Dressed up, sitting in a bar, sipping a drink with other well-dressed people, watching a normal-ish couple chained to a pillar and whipped. It's not your average evening, is it?

M. But does it turn you on?

F. No… It's amusing, I suppose. But can't say I'm getting aroused. How about you?

M. Well, I thought it might. The idea of it, you know? But here, in front of us. It just seems a bit sad. And kinda funny. Sad and funny, I guess.

A shift.

F. One of the waitresses looks like my sister. Something about the eyes. Accusatory.

M. Whack! They're really laying into them now. Taking it up a notch. Not holding back.

F. Pulls me out of this scene, puts me right back there. The look in their eyes just before I left. Her and Mam.

M. Whack! That actually has to hurt. No one is messing around here.

F. Running away, they said. Always the way. Not facing up to the shit with them. Legging it as usual.

M. Whack! How long will the marks from that last?

F. I think I faced enough. I think I faced as much of that shit as I could.

M. I'm not really sure anybody is enjoying this any more.

F. What am I going to do over there? It doesn't matter. I'll be over there. And away from all this. Forget all this.

M. Are you wondering why I brought you here?

F. Do other things. See other things. Be someone else. Who doesn't hurt like this.

M. Maybe I'm wondering that now.

F. But there's only so long that can last. Maybe they knew that. Maybe this waitress knows that. The way she's looking at me.

M. Seemed like the sort of thing you'd like to see. Everything that's different. Everything that's decadent.

F. Time to go back. Show them how I've changed.

M. Show you that I can be wild too. That I'm a part of this city now. All its eccentricities and excitements. They're me now too. I'm like this now.

F. Show them I'm ready to face all that shit with them. Show them I can stop running.

M. But am I, really? Is that something I want to be? Is that something you want me to be?

A shift.

F. You want to give it a go?

M. What?

F. Go next?

M. Up there?

F. Yeah.

M. Well, I…

F. Relax. I'm just messing with you. I'm not into exhibitionism.

M. Me neither.

F. They obviously are.

M. They're locked.

F. They don't seem that locked.

M. Maybe not. Their friends at the table seem to be enjoying it.

F. They look like normal office people.

M. Beers for the boys and cocktails for the girls.

F. The chained couple are stripped down to their underwear now.

M. They look so ordinary. Maybe they're here for someone's birthday.

F. Or an engagement party?

M. You think this would catch on back home?

F. Well, it's like everything else, isn't it? Only a matter of time…

M. Maybe…What time is it now?

F. Half twelve, why? You in a hurry somewhere?

M. You feel like dancing?

F. Always feel like dancing.

M. We're on the guestlist at Twilo till one. Sasha and Digweed.

F. Yeah? Class. Let's do it so.

M. So we drain our Masochists and it's *au revoir* to La Maison.

F. I link your arm and we pause outside the Chelsea Hotel.

M. You give me a quick kiss on the lips that I'm not expecting.

F. This is a really good night.

M. Yeah.

F. I'm having such a good time.

M. Good. Me too.

F. I really needed this… everything I'm going back to… This is a great blowout to say goodbye.

M. Goodbye?

F. To America. Top it off, you know?

M. Yeah, cool.

F. Thanks so much.

M. You lean in close to me again. I'm hoping for another kiss, but it's a hug this time.

F. And then we're walking again. Is it far?

M. Not far. Ten minutes maybe.

F. New York after midnight, as you would expect…

M. Police sirens in the distance.

F. The subway rumbling below.

M. High-lifers in taxicabs.

F. Low-lifers scurrying in the shadows.

M. Streets getting noticeably darker this way.

F. Down West 27th Street.

M. Way, way west, practically in view of the highway.

F. Past the longest nightclub queue I've ever seen.

M. Groups and groups of yoked-up ravers…

F. …complete with glowsticks and ultraviolet hair.

M. Chancin'-their-arm teenagers…

F. …and extras from *Mad Max*.

M. Besuited cokeheads and their blonde dates.

F. Chattering into their cellphones and handbags…

M.…and shivering against the shutters of garages and limo rental joints.

F. All waiting for entry to Twilo.

Twilo

M. Once again I marvel at the brilliance of being on the list.

F. As we stroll past all these less important punters and in through the roped-off entrance.

M. Depositing our coats with the smiley munchkin with the pawprint tit-tatts.

F. Then under the airport-style security arches.

M. And frisked by an enormous bouncer.

F. Can't be too careful.

M. All the while 'Out of Control' by the Chemical Brothers rumbles and builds around a bend up ahead.

F. Which we turn and head out on to the main floor of the club.

M. Dark and smoky, lit by lasers and blacklights and glowsticks and luminous expander spheres.

F. And basically any crazy shit that glows in the dark.

M. A full-on bouncy electro rave.

F. Everyone well into it.

M. Drugged up. Loved up. Fucked up.

F. Not giving a shit. Not pulling a pose.

M. Just dancing and dancing and sweating like fuck.

F. Class. Have to get some pills for this.

M. Really? I'm not so sure that's a good idea.

F. You're getting old.

M. Feel pretty far gone with all the alcohol, not sure I'm up for pills...

F. You don't want to do one. Not now? Not with me?

M. But you want to, so I'll do one, just to be on the same buzz, I guess. I watch you move across the dance floor.

F. Dancing through people. Free amongst the faces. Sweat and hair and arms flying. Everyone blissfully lost in the music.

M. You glide through them. So sexy. Neon-lit. Beautiful. I see guys and girls watching you. Thinking the same thing as me.

F. I pick one girl with closed eyes and willowy arms and ask her if she –

M. Yeah, she knows someone alright...

A shift.

F. And a little later, we're in a different part of the club.

M. Sofas, music lower, lights brighter, couples drinking and smoking, people talking. The chillout room.

F. But you're anything but. Sitting there. Smoking. Looking around. Your eyes narrow.

M. Insect-like. Reptile-like. Unblinking.

F. Just watching. Watching me. Watching everything.

M. Vision's all stuttery. Jumping in and out of focus. That's why I'm sitting. Everything else is too complicated. And that's why I'm smoking. The burning tip of the cigarette, something to focus on, something that's in my control.

F. I'm talking to the guy who sold me the ecstasy. He's a young Asian guy with blonde highlights. He's from Jersey and smiles a lot.

M. My eyes are slits. I am a reptile. I am a chameleon. Skin's tingling all over. Changing. Blending in with my surroundings. Disappearing from here, melting into the sofa. No one can see me. No one looking at me. No one talking to me. Not even you. I'm not here.

F. Breasts and spine starting to tingle with the mild come-up. I'm smiling too. The Asian guy talking about buses or something. Being a funny fuck. Still smiling. One tooth gold-plated.

M. I feel my long tongue flicking about inside my parched mouth. Coiled and ready to strike out at any of the brightly coloured insects around me. You're talking to one. A little down the sofa from me. Stuttery vision honed in on you. Every movement.

F. Not sure what he's telling me any more. But I'm laughing at whatever it is. Nodding to him. Looking down at my hands on my lap. My nails lightly tracing glowing orange trails over my bare thighs.

M. His eyes are watching your hands. Your thighs. You lean your face close to his ear. A whisper? What? He smiles, moves his head close to your ear, almost touching. I see his hand touch your thigh.

F. His hand is on my thigh. Cheeks twitch. Stuttery chemical rush behind my eyes.

M. Skin tingles painfully now. Some sort of madness burning up from inside. Camouflage disappears and I grow out of the couch.

F. All at once, a rush of displaced air and you're between us. Your face between us. Me and the smiling Asian guy from Jersey. Our faces lit faintly by the glow of your burning cigarette.

M. If you kiss her, I'll put this out on your fucking eyeball.

F. Asian guy's smile fades. Eyes widen. Turns to me.

M. I stare at him. Don't blink or breathe.

F. 'Sorry, didn't realise that was your girlfriend,' Asian guy says and backs away. Watching through lidded eyes and clotted mascara.

M. I rise with him, cigarette still poised, watch him disappear
into the crowd.

F. You sit back down beside me.

M. Did that just happen? Face is distorted in metal tabletop.
Doesn't look like me. Looks crazy. Someone else. Not me.

F. What's wrong with you? I wasn't gonna kiss him. He's gay.
I was just talking to him.

M. Don't say anything. Can't say anything.

F. Rushes turning to shivers. I can't look at you. Can't move.

M. You look in shock. I want you to be angry at me. To laugh at
me. Anything other than you looking so scared. Scared of me.

F. I need air.

M. You want to get out of here?

   A shift.

F. Ooh. Outside. The cool air sends chills through me. Sparking
the E off again. Pleasant, but indifferent. Pretty soft
indecisive yokes. Disappointing.

M. The breeze blowing down the street from the Hudson feels
good. Cools my tingling head. Turns my brain to liquid
mush. Escaping the shame for a while.

F. We head east toward 10th Avenue and somehow manage to
hail a cab at the corner.

M. St Mark's and First.

F. The taxi driver has a turban and an endless beard. He says
nothing and drives.

M. The bullet-proof partition between us. His stoic, dead-eyed
expression in the rear-view mirror. As Ricky Martin plays on
the shitty radio.

F. It doesn't take long till he drops us outside the Yaffa Café.

M. We get a tiny table by a painted statue of Buddha, under the
watchful eyes of dead Jim Morrison.

Yaffa

M. Have you talked to anyone from college the last while?

F. Apart from you?

M. Yeah.

F. No.

M. No one?

F. What's the point? Done with that. Finished. College friends are college friends. Don't mean that much, once you're through.

M. You won't stay friends with any of them?

F. Don't think so. Will you?

M. Yeah, I think so. Some of them.

F. I don't think you will.

M. Why?

F. Can't stay in contact with everyone you meet. Even good friends drift apart. Over time. Only natural. You do new things. Go new places. Meet new people.

M. That's depressing.

F. No, it's not.

M. It is. Three years in college with people you're never going to see again.

F. You'll pass them on the street. Dublin's small after all. The world's small too. Meet them on a beach in Thailand or Australia or something. Everyone ends up there eventually.

M. Thailand?

F. Australia. India. Wherever.

M. When did you get so cynical?

F. I think I was about… seven.

M. You don't think any of the college people are worth keeping in contact with?

F. No. What do we have in common now, except the past?

Pause.

You want to know why I was talking to that guy?

M. The guy in Twilo?

F. Yeah.

M. Why?

F. I wanted to get some coke. I felt like some coke.

M. And?

F. And he had some. He gave it to me. He was off his head. He gave it to me for nothing. 'Cause I'm Irish. 'Cause I'm fabulous. Something… You wanna do a line or two? Keep the come-down at bay?

M. We take turns in the tiny bathroom of the Yaffa, cutting out lines on the dirty toilet-roll dispenser.

F. Ever so glamorous this.

M. But fuck, a blast up either nostril gives me the jolt of life that I need right now.

F. Knocking the exhausted come-down feeling out of me and carrying me back to our little table feeling all sparkly again.

M. The room seems to shimmer around us.

F. Everything covered in glitter.

M. And the wine goes down in nice thick gulps.

F. And it's all smiles and rosy cheeks and excited chatter for a while.

M. Until you start to look a little yellow.

F. And your smile has been replaced by clenched teeth and your eyes are bloodshot and raw.

M. As the uncertainty creeps back.

I really freaked myself out by what I said to that guy in the club. That was just mental. I'm not like that. I'm not jealous. I just… I haven't seen you in so long and a lot of feelings

came back to me and the E was messing with my head and…
I'm really, really sorry.

F. Look, I said it was okay. Okay? You don't have to apologise
again. It was freaky, alright? You did scare me. But we're off
our faces. Mad shit happens. Let's just forget about it, okay?

M. Okay. It's forgotten.

F. Good.

M. And it is. We drink some coffee and share a slice of pie.

F. And do the rest of the coke.

M. The guilt I feel beginning to lessen.

F. I think the only other thing we can do tonight is go home and
pass out.

M. We pay the bill and leave.

Stairwell

F. Laughing, barely able to walk.

M. Crawling up the steps of my apartment building.

F. Starting to crash.

M. Hard. Someone's made gravity stronger.

F. Wasp nest where my brain should be. Stumbling through into
the narrow fluorescent hallway.

M. I catch you before you slide down the wall.

F. Laughing. Lost. Fucked. Pulling you towards me.

M. Kissing me.

F. Yeah and sort of passing out at the same time. Stars and shit
behind my eyelids. I open them. You're looking at me funny.
Disgust or worry?

M. There's blood. A dark crimson trail from your nostril to
your lips.

F. Shit.

M. Are you okay?

F. Do you have a tissue?

M. What happened?

F. It's okay. It's nothing.

M. Nothing? I give you a crumpled tissue from my jacket pocket. I think it's used but you don't seem to care.

F. Wipe away the blood. Laugh again. Stars again. Head back. Fucking beautiful.

M. Too much coke?

F. Too much of everything. You hold me and I lean in to you.

A shift.

M. What are you doing?

F. I'm dizzy.

M. No, I mean… pushing yourself this hard. Getting so fucked up.

F. You're not exactly sober yourself.

M. I'm going along with what you want.

F. What I want? I didn't want this. This was your idea. Your plan. Haven't seen each other in ages. Go partying. A night on the town.

M. Yeah, eat, drink, see some of the city.

F. So, what are you saying?

M. I don't know. Wasn't planning on doing… Getting this wrecked. You're bleeding. That's…

F. I'll be okay.

M. Will you?

F. What, you think I'm having some sort of breakdown or something?

M. No, I –

F. Me? I'm all here. I'm resilient. I'm wholesome, sweet, innocent. My daddy's little girl. His favourite.

M. But your daddy's dead now.

F. Yeah… So… I can do whatever I want. I can take care of myself.

M. You don't need any help?

F. You want to help me? You want to look after me?

M. Yes.

F. You're sweet.

M. Ouch. I'll be the one bleeding, you say that again.

F. Come on. Time for these fucking steps.

M. Almost there. Someone keeps adding extra flights to the stairwell.

F. At the top. You let go of me. Propped against the wall.

M. Fumbling with my keys. The flickering light outside my door has finally gave out.

F. I close my eyes and wait for the sound of the door opening.

M. But I don't open it because I'm looking at you.

F. What's left of me. A mess. I'm dissolving into this decrepit wallpaper. I can't open my eyes. My stomach is burning. I rub it.

M. You look out of focus. A smudged photograph. Your scruffy hands smooth the shimmering grey fabric of your dress.

F. A strange flash of memory makes me smile.

M. Slowly you slide the hem of your dress up your bare thighs.

F. I'm a child. A little girl. Six, seven, something. I'm happy. I'm sitting near the top of the stairs. I have my chubby legs through the bannisters. Mum and Dad are kissing below in the hall. In love. Kissing goodbye. I'm pressing myself against the bar, between my legs. It feels funny. Good. I laugh. Then and now.

M. Your dress is above your crotch now, you open your thighs. Exposing yourself to me further. I sink slowly to the cold tiles of the landing.

F. There's some trace of the ecstasy or maybe just the coke and alcohol circulating inside of me. A fuzzy liquid electricity that makes my skin shiver. Beautifully. To your touch. Your fingers on my calves.

M. And travelling slowly higher. Magnetised. The smell of you. Wine. Smoke. Sweat. Perfume. The heat from between your legs glowing close to my face. I close my eyes and sink into that warmth. Tasting you.

F. Disappearing completely. Melting into a puddle of chemicals. Natural and otherwise. Working their magic.

M. Dissolving into a warm, black, welcoming void.

M's Apartment

F. My mother told me: Don't trust men.

M. They only want your body.

F. And they only want it for a short time too.

M. Then they want someone else.

F. Don't trust them. Ever.

M. She's a wise woman.

F. Yes.

M. Think your dad only wanted her for her body?

F. She was good to him. She gave him everything. She gave him four daughters and one son.

M. Who's a little gone in the head.

F. You would be too if you had four sisters.

   Pause.

M. I think I love you.

F. You think?

M. I love you.

F. Don't say that.

M. It's what I feel.

F. You're still drunk. We've had sex. We're sleeping together.
I'm warm. Feel good beside you. That's what you feel.
That's all you feel.

M. I know what I feel. You're scared of that.

F. I'm not scared of anything.

M. What's wrong then?

F. I just don't want to hear that from you now.

M. Then when?

F. You hardly even know me.

M. What are you talking about? Of course I know you.

F. No, you don't.

M. I know you. Jesus, come on.

F. Why do you think you love me?

M. I don't think, I –

F. What is it about me you love?

M. You're different. You're special. Everyone else is so ordinary.

F. I'm not special. There's nothing special about me. I'm a
mess. I'm a waste.

M. What? You don't know yourself. I think you're perfect. I think
you're incredible. When you're not here, I keep seeing you.
I hear your voice in my head. Things you've said. Your voice.
Stored in there.

F. You're mad.

M. I know.

F. No, you're really crazy.

M. You're crazy. I can't believe you don't realise the effect you have on me.

F. I'm tired.

M. So am I.

F. Let's go to sleep.

M. You're afraid of getting hurt so you keep people at arm's length from you.

F. Go to sleep, please.

M. But the more you keep people at arm's length, the more you hurt them. And then you feel bad for doing that. So you push them away further, retreating back into your lonely armour of promiscuity and cynicism.

F. And you, what are you? You're seriously obsessive. You're selfish. Never shared your toys as a kid, huh? You want to hold on to everything, so tight. That's how you break things. Drain the life out of them. I don't like psychoanalysis. And this is giving me a headache.

M. You roll over.

F. Back to you.

M. Silence. Black, cold, silence.

F. You exaggerate. Time just passes. The room's warm, not cold. And New York is never silent.

M. I wasn't talking about the room or New York there.

A shift.

F. Colours and shapes begin to form behind my dark eyelids.

M. The street sounds outside change. Fade.

F. Merge. Swelling sounds. Waves. The sound of water. The ocean. Sounds in the centre of my head at first. And then all around me. By the ocean.

M. I'm holding your hand. Where are we? Moving downstairs. The stairwell. You're smiling at me. Happy. Fresh. Out on the dark street now. Moving through pools of light from the lamps. Night-time in New York.

F. Lying on a beach of soft white sand. Sun low in the sky in front of me. Setting. Tilting palms lilting behind me. A warm breeze through paradise. Thailand or somewhere I haven't been to yet. Yet here I am now. On the beach. By myself.

M. We're going down steps again. A subway station. Through the turnstiles and still holding your hand. Never letting go. Warm and clammy and familiar.

F. I say by myself but what I mean is, I am alone. There are many other people on the beach. But they are not with me. And the sun is definitely setting now, so people are starting to leave. But it's still almost perfect. Warm and shimmering and…

M. Inside on the platform. Eerily quiet. Echoes from the tunnel. We sit down on a bench together. Warm breeze from the tunnel mouth. Then footsteps. Voices. Three big guys. Blocking our exit. Scowling, grinning trouble. Shit.

F. My skin is different. Tanned, taut. Aged. Burned. Toughened. I'm older. A women. A middle-aged woman, lying here in the sun on this beach. In Thailand or wherever, I haven't been there yet.

M. They're up in our face now. You and me. We're standing now. Surrounded by these guys. Trying to talk with them. Reason with them. They want our money. They want what we have. We give it to them. But they want more. They shove me back onto the bench. A punch. A kick. One of them grabs your arm.

F. I watch a little blonde girl playing near the edge of the clear blue water. She splashes her hands in the sea, happily, laughing to herself. I feel my tired face spread into a smile and watch as she comes out of the sea and runs across the sand.

M. The two bigger guys are holding me down. Can't breathe. The smaller one, the leader, is pulling at your dress, off your shoulder, until – A fast vicious movement. You shove him, with all your strength, in the chest. He stumbles back off the edge of the platform.

F. The little girl runs past me. Her parents sitting up near the tree line. One of them seems… It's you. The little girl is your daughter. You sitting there on the sand. You look the same. As I remember you. You haven't aged.

M. He hits the tracks hard. His head clattering against the electric track. Sending volts and volts of electric blasts through his body. The other two release me to turn and watch their friend's body begin to smoke. His eyeballs explode with a wet pop.

F. You and your little women. Cute little daughter. Perfect little wife. Younger than me. She looks like she loves you more than breathing. A happy little unit. You don't recognise me. Don't even see me here. Staring until it hurts. Your happiness blinding me.

M. Your hand is suddenly in mine again, dragging me quickly from the bench and down the platform in a blur of frantic motion. You're so wild and strong and exciting. I'd do anything for you. Go anywhere with you. Escape all this. Together. To freedom. To paradise. Thailand, or somewhere... bright. So bright... as...

A shift.

F. Morning comes.

M. Breaking and entering through the bedroom window.

F. Muscling aside the venetian blinds and glaring up the room with white fire.

M. A dozen taxicabs honking away outside in a no-honking zone.

F. And construction workers drilling at a crack in the side of my skull.

M. Breakfast conversation is light and transparent.

F. Tired but friendly.

M. Making fun of the songs on the radio.

F. Not really looking at each other much.

M. And eating even less.

F. I dress in my travelling clothes while you're in the shower.

M. And we leave the apartment dazed and silent.

Park

F. It rains in the afternoon.

M. A heavy wet autumnal downpour.

F. You open up the umbrella and hold me close under it as we cross into the park.

M. Japanese tourists in plastic rain ponchos are taking photos of the John Lennon memorial.

F. Flowers of red and purple and yellow lay around the circular plaque, taking a heavy battering from the aggressive sheets of rain. Imagine.

M. We move down a curving path and follow the Park Drive for a while.

F. Then up a hill under a row of huge overhanging trees.

M. The trail we're on now is narrow and overgrown. It's amazing how quickly Central Park can become silent.

F. Rain's easing off, finding it harder to penetrate our canopy of thick branches.

M. I close the umbrella as you flop down onto a rotting bench by the side of the trail.

F. You sit down beside me.

M. You're crying.

F. It's raining.

M. Yeah, but you're crying too. Your eyes are red.

F. Daddy's little girl doesn't cry.

M. I don't think I've ever seen you cry. Not even…

F. I didn't have anything then. Not… the shock of it all. The bullshit. The…

M. It's okay.

F. But it's not.

Nothing makes sense any more. Nothing.

M. You don't say anything else for a while. I'm not sure how or
what I can reply. You look off away from me.

F. Not anything we did in college. Not anything since. Not
anything my family want me to do. None of it makes
any sense.

M. You don't know what to do?

F. Oh there's lots of things I can do. Things I *will* do. But I don't
think they'll change anything. Any of this.

M. Any of what? Your life? Who you are?

F. Any of the fucking nothing I feel now. That I've felt for as
long as I can remember. The, just, weight of nothingness.

M. You don't feel nothing.

F. Don't do that again. Don't tell me what I feel.

M. That's not what I was…

F. Alright.

M. You know, this is normal. This is what people can feel like
when…

F. None of this is normal. Nothing will ever be normal again.
If there ever was such a thing. Things change. Things end.
They never come back. Everyone moves on. Till they don't.

M. It's only a year.

F. A year. A whole year. Seems longer. Seems like yesterday.
I can barely remember what I was like before.

M. I can. And you'll be like that again.

F. No. It doesn't work like that.

    I miss him so fucking much.

M. I know.

F. I can't believe he left us here, just like that. It's not right.
No one was ready. No one knows what to do. How to…

M. You're doing as well as anyone. And you'll figure out the rest.

F. You don't understand. Not really. You can't.

M. I want to.

F. I know you do.

M. I want to help.

F. I know you do. I wish you could.

M. Fuck… You're wiping your eyes dry. I look away. You hate me seeing you like this. I try to put an arm around you.

F. But I shrug it off. I'm okay. You didn't need to hear any of that.

M. It's okay.

F. I shouldn't have said any of that. It's pathetic.

M. No.

F. I know it is. Fucking bullshit on top of bullshit.

M. No.

F. Promise me you'll never tell anyone I was like this. Ever.

M. Why would I?

F. Promise.

M. I promise.

Your tears are gone. Cheeks pale. You stand up from the bench.

F. Rain's easing off.

M. We walk on along the trail in silence for a while.

F. As we emerge from the awning of trees into the open again you put the umbrella back up and attempt to hug me closer under it.

M. But you shrug my arm off your shoulder again and move a little ahead of me.

F. It's okay, it's not really raining any more.

Museum

M. On the east side of Central Park is the Metropolitan Museum of Art.

F. Inside the museum is very busy. Lots of children and tourists.

M. We wander around the massive building in a daze.

F. Not bothering with any map, we move from room to room.

M. Glancing dreamily at the paintings and statues.

F. Pausing every once in a while to examine pieces that we recognise.

M. Downstairs is a reconstructed Egyptian temple.

F. Dedicated to Isis and Osiris, the Temple of Dendur.

M. As we look down into the reflecting pool around the temple, I smile and reach out to take your hand.

F. Without looking at you, I slip my hand free and move on.

M. We move on through a hall of various armour from around the world. I can't stop thinking about why you won't hold my hand. About what you told me in the park.

F. Behind me you stop and sit down opposite a large samurai.

M. I squeeze my throat. The back of it is hard and dry.

F. Why did you stop?

M. I don't know.

F. Are you okay?

M. I'm fine. Just a little tired.

F. I thought…

M. What?

F. I was after upsetting you or something. I thought you were… crying?

M. No, just… tired.

F. You smile and get up from the bench, walking alongside me again.

It's closing time soon.

M. Yeah.

F. We should go.

M. Yeah.

F. Let's go.

M. Okay.

Crossing Again

M. Walking today. Just walking. No hurry. No particular destination. Hand-in-hand with my –

F. What's your girlfriend like?

M. I don't have a girlfriend.

F. Yes, you do.

M. I do?

F. You forget? Today? I saw you with her. I saw you. You let go of her hand for an instant.

M. Yes. She's…

F. Like me in some ways? But so different also…

M. Hey.

F. Hi.

M. No more.

F. Just that.

M. Then moving past.

F. No more.

A shift.

M. You've tainted me.

F. I have?

M. You've changed me.

F. I didn't mean to.

M. Nothing is the same after you. You're the one that all others are compared to.

F. You did that. Not me.

M. Maybe...

F. Don't blame me. You can't blame me for your...

M. What?

F. She's about as attractive as you. About as normal. About as fucked up. About as boring. About as interesting. About as...

M. Yes.

F. You're well-suited.

M. We are.

F. For each other.

M. We could be... We are.

F. Happy?

M. Yes.

F. Overrated?

M. I don't know...

A shift.

I had to say that to you last night. That is how I feel.

F. I know.

M. And you don't...

F. I'm sorry...

M. Don't be.

Pause.

F. It was a great weekend.

M. Memorable?

F. Yes.

M. Still there…

F. Still holding tight.

> *A shift.*

M. So many places we've been have gone. That restaurant.
La Maison de Sade. Twilo. Gone. Changed. Disappeared.
No more.

F. That's what happens. That's life. Loss. Change. Stop holding
so tight. Let me go.

M. I don't know who you are any more. Not really. I see you
then. On the street. What sort of life have you had? Since…

F. I'm not even a real person to you any more.

M. No. The colour of your eyes. The sound of your voice. What
you said to me. Have I changed them?

F. An idea of a person.

M. An obsession. A fantasy. A dream.

F. Let go.

M. A moment. Too long.

F. Until boarding is announced.

M. This is not the last time I'll see you.

F. But it is the last time I'll speak to you.

M. The last time I'll hold you.

F. Is this all it was?

M. A brief stopover?

F. On the way from somewhere.

M. To someplace else.

F. Another time and place entirely.

M. Is this all it was?

F. Well, it's still here…

M. We're still there… How real was this?

F. You say goodbye.

M. I say… I say… I stay.

The End

A Nick Hern Book

Stop/Over first published as a single edition in Great Britain in 2018 as a paperback original by Nick Hern Books Limited, The Glasshouse, 49a Goldhawk Road, London W12 8QP, in association with On The Quays

An earlier version of the play was first published as part of *Irish Shorts* in 2013 by Nick Hern Books

Stop/Over copyright © 2018 Gary Duggan

Gary Duggan has asserted his right to be identified as the author of this work

Cover photograph by David Cleary

Designed and typeset by Nick Hern Books, London
Printed in Great Britain by Mimeo Ltd, Huntingdon, Cambridgeshire PE29 6XX

A CIP catalogue record for this book is available from the British Library

ISBN 978 1 84842 811 9